Wars Waged Under the Microscope

The War Against the Flu

Louise Spilsbury

CRABTREE
PUBLISHING COMPANY
WWW.CRABTREEBOOKS.COM

CRABTREE
PUBLISHING COMPANY
WWW.CRABTREEBOOKS.COM

Author: Louise Spilsbury

Editors: Sarah Eason, Jennifer Sanderson, and Ellen Rodger

Editorial director: Kathy Middleton

Design: Simon Borrough

Cover design and additional artwork: Katherine Berti

Photo research: Rachel Blount

Proofreader: Wendy Scavuzzo

Production coordinator and Prepress technician: Ken Wright

Print coordinator: Katherine Berti

Consultant: David Hawksett

Produced for Crabtree Publishing by Calcium Creative Ltd

Library and Archives Canada Cataloguing in Publication

Title: The war against the flu / Louise Spilsbury.
Names: Spilsbury, Louise, author.
Description: Series statement: Wars waged under the microscope | Includes bibliographical references and index.
Identifiers: Canadiana (print) 20210189142 | Canadiana (ebook) 20210189150 |
  ISBN 9781427151339 (hardcover) |
  ISBN 9781427151414 (softcover) |
  ISBN 9781427151490 (HTML) |
  ISBN 9781427151575 (EPUB)
Subjects: LCSH: Influenza—Juvenile literature. | LCSH: Influenza—Treatment—Juvenile literature. | LCSH: Influenza—Prevention—Juvenile literature. | LCSH: Epidemics—Juvenile literature.
Classification: LCC RC150 .S65 2022 | DDC j614.5/18—dc23

Library of Congress Cataloging-in-Publication Data

Names: Spilsbury, Louise, author.
Title: The war against the flu / Louise Spilsbury.
Description: New York, NY : Crabtree Publishing Company, [2022] | Series: Wars waged under the microscope | Includes index.
Identifiers: LCCN 2021016656 (print) | LCCN 2021016657 (ebook) |
  ISBN 9781427151339 (hardcover) |
  ISBN 9781427151414 (paperback) |
  ISBN 9781427151490 (ebook) |
  ISBN 9781427151575 (epub)
Subjects: LCSH: Influenza--Juvenile literature. | Influenza--Treatment--Juvenile literature. | Influenza--Prevention--Juvenile literature. | Epidemics--Juvenile literature.
Classification: LCC RC150 .S69 2022 (print) | LCC RC150 (ebook) | DDC 616.2/03--dc23
LC record available at https://lccn.loc.gov/2021016656
LC ebook record available at https://lccn.loc.gov/2021016657

Crabtree Publishing Company
www.crabtreebooks.com   1-800-387-7650

Printed in the U.S.A./062021/CG20210401

Published in Canada
Crabtree Publishing
616 Welland Ave.
St. Catharines, Ontario
L2M 5V6

Published in the United States
Crabtree Publishing
347 Fifth Ave.
Suite 1402-145
New York, NY 10016

Contents

The Enemy

According to the **World Health Organization (WHO)**, each year, influenza, or the flu, makes as many as 5 million people severely sick and causes up to 650,000 deaths around the world. The flu is caused by **viruses** that attack a person's nose, throat, and lungs. People who have the flu may cough and sneeze a lot, and have muscle aches and pains.

Flu as the Enemy

The flu is often only a mild disease. However, it is very contagious, which means it spreads easily from person to person. As a result of this, it can cause epidemics. An epidemic is when thousands of people in a community or country catch a disease at the same time. Pandemics are epidemics that spread through many different countries. For example, the 1918 pandemic (sometimes called the Spanish flu) infected about 500 million people. It killed at least 50 million people worldwide.

*This is what a single influenza virus may look like under a **microscope**. Tiny though it is, the virus can turn the body into a factory that spreads the disease once it gets inside.*

Pr. Doctor Schna- -bel von

In the 1400s, doctors were so fearful of diseases such as the flu that they wore protective clothing while treating patients, including a beak-like mask, shown left.

The Story of the Flu

In the past, doctors came up with many different explanations for how the flu came about. In the 1300s, people in Florence, Italy, explained an **outbreak** of the flu as *influenza di freddo*, which translates to "influenced by the cold." Then in 1414, when an epidemic in France affected 100,000 people in the capital city, Paris, doctors there believed a smelly and cold wind caused people's flu **symptoms**. By the 1700s, the word "influenza" was commonly used to describe the disease. However, at the time, people believed cold air caused the illness.

> *There was a little girl, and she had a little bird,*
> *And she called it by the pretty name of Enza;*
> *But one day it flew away but it didn't go to stay,*
> *For when she raised the window, in-flu-Enza.*
>
> **Childhood chant from 1918**

The Battle Begins

People did not begin to fully understand what caused influenza until the early 1900s, when a deadly strain spread across the world. The 1918 pandemic caused so many people to die that medical science began a dedicated effort to learn more about this enemy.

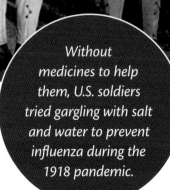

Without medicines to help them, U.S. soldiers tried gargling with salt and water to prevent influenza during the 1918 pandemic.

Searching for the Virus

In 1918, most scientists believed that influenza was caused by bacteria. Bacteria are single-celled **organisms** that can cause disease. However, the scientists and doctors had not been able to find identical bacteria in **samples** taken from a range of flu patients. So, they started to search instead for something they called a virus.

In the early 1930s, Richard Shope, a doctor from Iowa, isolated, or separated, the flu virus from swine, or pigs, infected with a highly contagious flu-like disease. The disease symptoms were so similar to human influenza that it was named swine influenza.

What Caused Swine Flu?

To figure out what was causing swine flu, Richard Shope took bacteria from the spit of a sick pig and injected them into a healthy pig. When the second pig did not become sick, he knew the flu was not an infection caused by bacteria. He then took the bacteria out of the pig spit and injected the remaining substance into the healthy pig. The pig became sick, proving that something other than bacteria caused the disease.

Identifying the Enemy

Shope's finding was quickly followed by the isolation of the influenza virus from humans by a team of **virologists** at the National Institute for Medical Research in the United Kingdom (UK). In 1933, Wilson Smith, Christopher Andrewes, and Patrick Laidlaw transferred human **antigens**, which were not bacteria, to ferrets. The ferrets became infected with the flu. This helped the team identify the antigen as a virus. A virus was described as an antigen that was too small to be seen. It could be filtered, and still produced disease, even though it could not reproduce on its own.

Today, thermal cameras can be used to detect pigs that have a high body temperature and therefore are likely to have swine flu.

An Invisible Threat

Once scientists had identified the flu virus, the next step was to discover how it got inside cells and caused disease. They were then able to understand how the virus spread.

Virus Invasion

When a virus invades a body, it seeks out cells and moves inside them. Once inside a cell, a virus uses the cell to replicate, or make copies of itself, so it can spread rapidly to other cells throughout the body. Once the virus has done this, it can spread to other people.

Virus All Around

When someone coughs or sneezes, viruses from their mouth and nose can travel through the air around them, where other people breathe them in. Traces of the flu virus can also be left on surfaces, such as a phone or doorknob, when someone who is sick touches them. When another person touches those objects and then their eyes, nose, or mouth, the virus enters their body and makes them sick.

The flu spreads from person to person through actions such as sneezing, coughing, and touching.

Being Contagious

A person who has the flu can pass on the virus before they even feel sick. Once they feel sick, they remain contagious for several days. Most people begin to show symptoms of the flu within two days of coming into contact with the virus. They then become contagious within three to four days of becoming sick. However, some people may be contagious just one day after catching the flu, before they even begin to show symptoms of the illness.

Washing hands in warm, soapy water for 20 seconds is one of the most effective ways to stop the flu virus from spreading. It is especially important to wash hands before eating food or touching the eyes, nose, or mouth because these are routes that viruses can take into a person's body.

Regular handwashing is important not only to keep from getting the flu but also to prevent passing it to other people.

"*When you wash your hands, you can prevent...1 in 5 **respiratory** infections such as a cold or flu.*"

Centers for Disease Control and Prevention (CDC)

Under Attack

When a flu virus takes hold, it is as though the body is under attack. The virus infects the **respiratory tract**, which is the part of the body that includes the nose, throat, and lungs. Air passes through the respiratory tract when people inhale, or take in breath.

Feeling Fluey

Flu symptoms come on very quickly and may only last a week or two. However, they can be very uncomfortable, and in some cases, deadly. Flu symptoms can include a sudden fever, which is when the body gets too hot and cannot cool down. Aches and pains, a dry cough, a sore throat, sneezing, a stuffy nose, and a headache are also common symptoms. People who have the flu often feel very tired, but may have difficulty sleeping. They may lose their appetite and not feel like eating or drinking. This can leave them feeling weak and exhausted.

The flu can be unpleasant, but if someone is otherwise healthy, it will usually clear up within a week or two.

White blood cells are part of the **immune system**. They can attack antigens. Antigens are substances such as the flu virus that, if they get into the body, cause the immune system to respond. In an **immunoglobulin** test, doctors use a microscope to measure the levels of **antibodies** in the blood. Low levels of antibodies mean a person is at risk from disease.

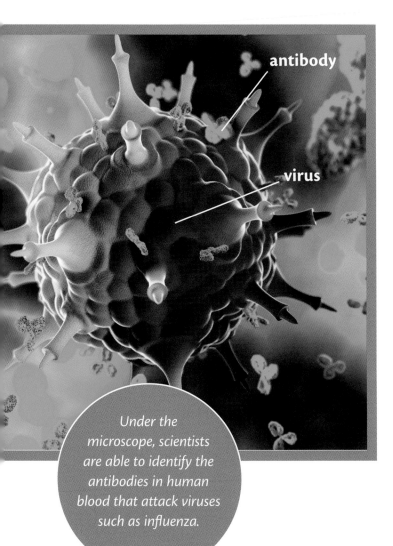

antibody

virus

Under the microscope, scientists are able to identify the antibodies in human blood that attack viruses such as influenza.

What Makes Flu Deadly?

Usually, someone with the flu does not need extensive medical treatment. In most cases, they will make a quick recovery. However, the sickness can become deadly if someone with the flu develops a **secondary infection** such as pneumonia. Pneumonia is an infection that inflames the air sacs, or tiny sacks that fill with air, in the lungs. It leaves people with a very high temperature, uncomfortable coughing, chills, and difficulty breathing. People at high risk from the flu are those with a weak immune system. This includes children under five years old, pregnant women, those with **asthma**, and the elderly, who may have weakened respiratory systems.

Epidemics and Pandemics

Epidemics and pandemics usually happen when a new type of influenza virus emerges, against which the immune system has no defense. This virus is able to infect people easily and spreads very quickly.

No Defenses

White blood cells in the body's immune system help defend against some recurring diseases. These are diseases that attack the body more than once. There are two basic types of antigen-fighting cells. **Phagocytes** attack invading antigens. **Lymphocytes** allow the body to remember and recognize previous invaders. However, when a new type of influenza virus hits, no one has immunity, or an immune system that can protect them from the disease. This is because their bodies have not encountered it before. This allows the virus to affect more people and to spread quickly through populations and across countries, causing epidemics and pandemics.

When someone with the flu travels, they take the influenza virus with them and risk spreading it to people in other countries.

CASE STUDY: 1889 RUSSIAN FLU

Before equipment such as microscopes could help, studying similarities between pandemics was an important way to learn about them. The 1889 Russian flu was the first flu pandemic that scientists had a lot of information about. The outbreak began in Russia, but soon spread to most European capital cities. Several waves of Russian flu occurred, which together killed more than 1 million people.

At that time, the doctors did not know they were dealing with the flu. Instead, many believed the disease was caused by miasmas, which is rotting **organic** matter carried through the air. The speed with which the disease spread appeared to provide evidence that this was the case. However, some doctors believed that the disease was contagious and that it spread between people. There was evidence that it moved most rapidly through railroad and postal workers because they came into contact with more people. With no real idea about its cause, doctors were unable to stop it. Only later did people learn that the outbreak was caused by the flu virus. They named the outbreak the Great Russian Flu Pandemic.

TOUT LE MONDE L'A (ter) L'INFLUENZA!

des Médecins et des Potards.

This cartoon from the Russian flu pandemic shows a patient being swept along by skeletons, surrounded by helpless doctors, and offered useless medicines.

Studying the Enemy

When scientists saw the flu virus for the first time in the 1930s, it was thanks to the invention of the **electron** microscope. Electron microscopes use a beam of electrons to help scientists examine objects in far greater detail than a conventional, or regular, microscope. Electron microscopes have proven to be valuable in the fight against tiny enemies such as the flu virus.

This is an electron micrograph image of an influenza virus. Colors have been added to help show its fine details.

Close-up on the Virus

When scientists began to use the electron microscope, they could see flu viruses in a cell and identify them by their shape and structure. Some flu viruses look like football-shaped pincushions, with a thick envelope spiked with tiny rods. This helped the scientists figure out how an influenza virus invades and takes over the parts of a body cell that make it work. They also learned how the flu virus can replicate its own genome. A genome is a set of instructions for living things called genes, made up of a chemical code called **DNA**. Influenza genes are written in a code similar to DNA, called **ribonucleic acid (RNA)**.

Different Types of Influenza Virus

Scientists also discovered there were different types of influenza viruses. By the 1940s, they had isolated and identified two main types: A and B. Later, they found C and D and **subtypes** such as H1N1 and H5N1. These were so-named because the surface of influenza virus **particles** is covered in small **proteins** called hemagglutinin (HA) and neuraminidase (N). These can mutate, or change, rapidly, and these changes result in a new type of flu virus.

UNDER THE MICROSCOPE

Today, doctors can carry out a rapid flu test. First, they use a **swab** to collect a sample of **mucus** or other fluids from the nose or throat. Then they do a test that can detect the antigens of influenza viruses in 10 minutes. However, this is not the most accurate test. A more accurate test is when a doctor takes a sample of **tissue**, blood, or other fluid (such as spinal fluid) to repeat the test in detail and looks for the DNA or RNA of a specific virus under a microscope.

This doctor is using a swab to take a sample from a patient's throat that can be tested for influenza antigens.

Tracking the Enemy

One factor that makes it difficult to identify and study flu viruses is that new forms of the flu can sometimes transfer from animal to human populations. Researchers are still unsure exactly how this transfer takes place, but they identify the virus and its specific mutations by first identifying its genome.

To guard themselves from the Swine Flu Pandemic of 2009–2010, people wore masks when in public.

Sequencing a Genome

A genome can be identified by a method that is sometimes called reverse genetics. First, scientists figure out the sequence in a virus's genome. They use that to reproduce its RNA, then add that to cells. The cells produce thousands of viral particles. This allows researchers to study the virus to see which parts of the genome make them more or less deadly. For example, the virus that caused the Swine Flu Pandemic of 2009–2010 contained a unique combination of influenza genes not previously identified in animals or humans. The virus was named influenza A (H1N1)pdm09.

CASE STUDY: TRACING THE SPANISH FLU

The 1918 pandemic killed 72 of the 80 adult villagers living in an oceanside village in Alaska called Brevig Mission. They were buried together in a mass grave. Through the years, the grave remained frozen because it was in an area of **permafrost**. The permafrost preserved, or kept from rotting, the tissue of the buried bodies.

The 1918 pandemic killed almost all the people of Brevig Mission in five days.

In 1951, Johan Hultin, a scientist from the University of Iowa, was given permission to take samples of frozen tissue from the dead villagers. He hoped to find the Spanish flu virus. Once back in Iowa, the tissue was injected into animals in the hope that they would catch the 1918 virus. However, the experiment failed because the virus was not alive.

Fast-forward to 1997 when Jeffery Taubenberger, a scientist working for the Armed Forces Institute of Pathology in Washington, DC, was working on sequencing the genome of the 1918 virus. Hultin returned to Alaska to get lung tissue from Brevig Mission victims. He gave it to Taubenberger to help him rebuild the genes in the virus's makeup. The two scientists learned from the reconstructed sequence that the 1918 flu virus probably got the protein from farm and wild birds that helped its genes mutate. Thanks to this work, by 2005, the genome of the 1918 influenza virus was sequenced.

Armed with Medicine

Identifying the flu virus was incredibly important because it allowed scientists to come up with vaccines. Vaccines are medicines that prevent a virus from multiplying and can help people recover from the flu more quickly.

The First Vaccines

In the mid-1930s, after the influenza A virus was identified, researchers began working on flu vaccines. A vaccine contains a harmless form of a virus, which is usually injected into the body to encourage the blood to make antibodies. The antibodies defend against the actual virus. Many soldiers had died from flu during **World War I**, so the U.S. military was eager to test a new vaccine on soldiers fighting in **World War II**. This first flu vaccine was tested in 1940 and was a success.

This lab technician is preparing a needle with a flu vaccine to protect American servicemen and women against the flu.

Fighting Different Forms

After the influenza B virus was discovered in 1940, a new vaccine was made in 1942. It covered the A and B viruses. In 1945, the vaccine was used on civilians, or nonmilitary people. But, in 1947, the same vaccine completely failed during a **seasonal** flu epidemic. Scientists then realized that there are many forms of flu virus, so it would be very hard to treat influenza with just one vaccine.

UNDER THE MICROSCOPE

Making vaccines against the flu requires a simple way of growing large amounts of flu viruses. In 1931, American doctor Ernest William Goodpasture invented methods of growing viruses in chicken eggs. In the 1940s, other scientists built on Goodpasture's work, especially in the U.S. military, which developed the first approved vaccines for influenza. Their vaccine used chicken eggs in a method that is still used to produce most flu vaccines today.

Scientists use a small needle to punch a hole in the top of a chicken egg. This creates a hole for the influenza virus to be injected into the egg.

Taking It to the Front Line

Around the world, scientists are researching influenza viruses and vaccines. In 1948, the WHO set up the Influenza Centre in London, UK, to collect and study influenza viruses. In 1952, it added a network of laboratories around the world to study how influenza viruses change over time.

Annual Vaccines

Scientists use the best information available to figure out how to make flu vaccines. As many strains of the virus exist and they are constantly mutating, new influenza vaccines must be made every year. The seasonal flu vaccine is changed every year to keep up with the particular strains of influenza viruses that research suggests will be most common in the following year. Some people are offered a vaccine given as a nasal, or nose, spray. Other vaccines are injected.

This lab technician in China is carrying out tests to figure out what vaccines will be most effective in the coming flu season.

Antiviral Drugs

It is difficult to develop drugs that can kill viruses. This is because the virus takes over part of a cell to replicate, so destroying the virus could destroy the cell, too. Antivirals are drugs that, rather than kill viruses, stop them from replicating instead. Antivirals are **prescription** medicines in the form of pills, liquid, or a powder, which fight against the flu. Antiviral treatment works best when started within two days of developing flu symptoms. Antiviral drugs are flu treatments but not cures. They work by lowering the fever and lessening other symptoms. They can also shorten the time people are sick with the flu by about one day. They may prevent serious flu complications, such as pneumonia.

"

"What's unique about influenza is it's constantly changing. We're really concerned about being ahead of the game for detecting a virus that could cause the next global pandemic."

Dr. Jacqueline Katz, Director of the WHO's Collaborating Center for the Surveillance, Epidemiology and Control of Influenza, Atlanta, Georgia, 2018

"

Fighting Back

Scientists are constantly tracking the flu virus to watch for mutations. Influenza viruses change in two main ways. Antigenic drift happens when a few mutations develop in an influenza genome and lead to seasonal changes. Antigenic shift happens when two influenza strains recombine their genomes to make a form previously unknown in humans. A pandemic happens after an antigenic shift and is usually linked to the influenza A virus.

Animal vaccines do not protect against all types of the flu because flu viruses constantly change. Scientists keep a constant lookout for variant viruses that could infect humans.

Zoonotic Diseases

Infections that spread from animals to people and cause diseases are described as zoonotic diseases or zoonoses. Around the world, scientists monitor reports and cases of bird flu and other forms of animal flu to learn if they could be a zoonotic disease. When an influenza A virus that spreads in animals infects a person, it is called a variant virus infection. Experts investigate reports of variant virus outbreaks to ensure these viruses are not changing in ways that would allow them to spread easily among people and cause an epidemic.

CASE STUDY: THE 2009-2010 SWINE FLU PANDEMIC

On April 17, 2009, an influenza A (H1N1) virus was detected in the United States. By June 2009, a total of 74 countries and territories had reported confirmed infections. This was the first global flu pandemic in 40 years.

On April 24, the CDC in the United States uploaded genomes of the H1N1 virus to an international **database.** This meant that scientists around the world could identify it and share information. The sharing of information paid off. By May 1, 2009, the CDC had identified that the 2009 H1N1 influenza virus contained virus genes from four different influenza virus sources. Some came from North American pig flu viruses, while others came from North American bird flu viruses. Another came from a human flu virus and two were normally found in pig flu viruses from Asia and Europe. It took almost four months for scientists to prepare a vaccine for the virus.

This doctor is examining a flu patient for signs of swine flu at a clinic in Mexico City in 2009.

New Weapons

In the future, the world's ability to tackle the flu and possible pandemics depends on locating and identifying zoonotic influenza viruses early. Scientists inventing new and improved antiviral drugs and vaccines will be just as important in the fight.

New Antivirals

The antiviral drugs used today can stop the flu virus from multiplying. But, for the best results, most must be taken within two days of contracting, or catching, the flu. They also only reduce the length of the illness by about 24 hours. Scientists are trying to develop new antiviral drugs, which, when used alongside other drugs, could help cut the amount of virus that is present in patients who have influenza A.

A virologist examines the results of an HI test. HI tests can tell people whether antibodies, developed through vaccination, will also recognize new flu viruses.

Many virologists hope that in the near future, a universal vaccine will be able to greatly reduce a person's flu symptoms, even if it cannot get rid of the influenza virus altogether.

Improved Vaccines

To be prepared for future zoonotic influenza outbreaks, scientists are aiming to develop more candidate vaccine viruses (CVVs) for new bird flu viruses. A CVV is an influenza virus that has been prepared by a public health organization. A CVV can be used by drug companies to produce a flu vaccine. Other scientists are working on a universal influenza vaccine. This is a vaccine that can be given just once and provides protection against the flu year after year.

Making a universal vaccine relies on targeting a part of the virus that does not change much. However, that is not how vaccines are usually made. Annual flu vaccines target particular proteins on the surface of a flu virus, but these are constantly changing. If you think of the flu virus as a ball with a lot of popsicles on sticks jutting out, the popsicles themselves are the proteins that constantly change, but the sticks remain the same.

Although scientists are focusing on the "sticks" as a target for a universal flu vaccine, it will probably be many years before a universal vaccine is available. When this vaccine is developed, it will be of extraordinary significance in the battle against the flu.

Future Warfare

Today, there are more tools to combat flu pandemics than ever before. As well as global influenza **surveillance** systems and the sharing of influenza virus information, scientists are learning to make new vaccines and antivirals more quickly. However, there is always a risk that the influenza virus could find ways to resist new vaccines. Everyone must do all they can in the battle against this microscopic enemy.

Flu droplets fly out when people cough or sneeze, so covering coughs and sneezes is one thing everyone can do to stop the flu from spreading.

Being Prepared

Scientists routinely develop CVVs for viruses such as new bird flu viruses. This is because bird flu viruses are becoming more common and could cause a pandemic in the future. Data collected through worldwide animal flu surveillance is used to select the CVVs. These potential vaccines are kept in stock and ready to use against animal flu viruses that might pose a risk to human health.

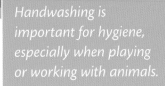

Handwashing is important for hygiene, especially when playing or working with animals.

Prevention Is Better Than a Cure

In 2017, the CDC updated guidelines for prevention measures for flu pandemics, based on the latest scientific evidence. These include actions that people can take to help slow the spread of the flu, such as staying home when sick, coughing or sneezing into a tissue, and frequently washing hands. Most human infections with new influenza A viruses have happened after close contact with infected animals. Examples of preventions for zoonotic diseases include checking animal health at farm shows or animal fairs, contacting a veterinarian when animals show signs of illness, isolating sick animals, and teaching people the importance of handwashing after being around animals.

"When we think of the major threats...another kind of threat lurks beyond our shores, one from nature, not humans—an **avian** flu pandemic."

Barack Obama, president of the United States 2009–2017

Timeline

Knowing that influenza is caused by a virus has helped doctors and scientists to understand the illness and to find ways to treat it. Scientists are always working to develop technology to learn about this deadly enemy.

1414 A flu epidemic in France is believed to be caused by a smelly and cold wind.

1700s The word "influenza" is used to describe the disease, and most people think it is caused by the cold.

1889 The Russian flu kills more than 1 million people.

1918 The Spanish Flu Pandemic kills at least 50 million people worldwide.

1931 The electron microscope is invented.

1933 First isolation of influenza, proving that it is caused by a virus not a bacterium.

1936 The influenza virus is grown in chicken eggs.

1940 Influenza B viruses are discovered.

1940s A vaccine for the influenza virus is made and given to soldiers fighting in World War II.

1945 Flu vaccines are given to nonmilitary people.

1947   The first flu vaccine fails during a seasonal flu epidemic.

1948   The WHO sets up an Influenza centre to collect and study influenza viruses.

1952   The WHO establishes a network of laboratories to study how influenza viruses change over time.

1997   FluNet, a web-based flu surveillance tool, is launched by the WHO for tracking the movement of flu viruses.

1998   Influenza virus surveillance in swine, conducted by the United States Department of Agriculture (USDA), begins in the United States.

2005   The genome of the 1918 Spanish Flu Pandemic virus is fully sequenced.

2009–2010   The Swine Flu Pandemic affects 74 countries.

2017   The CDC updates guidelines for prevention measures for flu pandemics.

Glossary

antibodies Substances produced by the body that fight off invading bacteria and viruses

antigens Invaders in the body, such as viruses

asthma A long-term condition that affects the tubes used in breathing

avian Of, or relating to, birds

cells The smallest units of living things that can survive on their own, carrying out a range of life processes

database An organized collection of data stored on a computer

DNA Deoxyribonucleic acid—a part of the body's cells that gives each individual their own unique characteristics

electron An extremely small piece of matter with a negative electrical charge

immune system The organs and other parts of the body that work together to protect it against sickness

immunoglobulin A protein produced by the body that can attack harmful bacteria and viruses in the body

lymphocytes Types of white blood cells that allow the body to remember and recognize previous invaders

microscope An instrument that uses special lenses to magnify, or make very small things large enough to see

mucus A slimy substance made by the body

organic Relating to living things

organisms Living things

outbreak Infection of more than one person

particles Tiny, independent pieces

permafrost Ground that remains frozen all year round

phagocytes Types of white blood cell that attacks invading antigens

prescription Describes medicines that are ordered by doctors for their patients

proteins The substances that do most of the work in cells

respiratory Describing the organs that allow a person to breathe and exchange oxygen and carbon dioxide throughout the body

respiratory tract The passage formed by the mouth, nose, throat, and lungs, through wich breathing occurs

ribonucleic acid (RNA) A substance that, in some viruses, carries the information that allows the virus to replicate

samples Small amounts of something, such as blood, for testing

secondary infection An infection resulting from another infection

seasonal Related to the seasons

subtypes Special types included within a more general type

surveillance Close observation

swab An absorbent pad that can be used by doctors to take samples

symptoms Signs of illness

tissue A group of cells of the same type, such as muscle cells, that perform a job together

virologists Scientists who study viruses

viruses Microscopic organisms that can cause sickness

World Health Organization (WHO) An organization that helps governments improve their health services

World War I The war fought from 1914 to 1918 mainly in Europe and the Middle East

World War II The war fought from 1939 to 1945 in which the Allies (including Britain, the Soviet Union, and the United States) defeated the Axis powers (including Germany, Italy, and Japan)

Learning More

Find out more about the flu and how the war against this disease is being won.

Books

Brown, Don. *Fever Year: The Killer Flu of 1918*. HMH Books for Young Readers, 2019.

Goh, Hwee. *Invisible Enemies: A Handbook on Pandemics That Have Shaped Our World*. Marshall Cavendish International, 2020.

Hand, Carol. *The Gross Science of Germs All Around You* (Way Gross Science). Rosen Central, 2018.

Krasner, Barbara. *Influenza: How the Flu Changed History* (Infected!). Capstone Press, 2019.

McCoy, Erin L. *Deadly Viruses* (Top Six Threats to Civilization). Cavendish Square, 2019.

Websites

There is a simple explanation of viruses and a diagram at:
https://kids.britannica.com/kids/article/virus/390098

Read facts about the flu and what to do if you get it at:
https://kidshealth.org/en/teens/flu-center/about-flu?ref=search

Learn more about influenza viruses at:
www.cdc.gov/flu/resource-center/freeresources/graphic-novel/EducationalOverview_v2.pdf

Watch animations of how vaccines work at:
www.historyofvaccines.org/content/how-vaccines-work

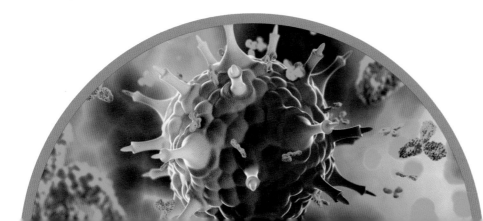

Index

ABOUT THE AUTHOR

Award-winning author Louise Spilsbury, who also writes under the name Louise Kay Stewart, has written more than 250 books for young people on a wide range of subjects. When not tapping away at her computer keys, she loves swimming in the sea and making bonfires on the beach near her home.